PYX

PENGUIN BOOKS

PYX

Corinne Lee's poems have been published in dozens of online and print literary magazines, ranging from the *Beloit Poetry Journal* to *Fine Madness*. Ms. Lee has been a multiple nominee for the Pushcart Prize. She was educated at the Iowa Writers' Workshop and the Radcliffe Publishing Institute. Winnow Press, her publishing company, specializes in emerging poets and fiction writers (www.winnowpress.com). Ms. Lee lives in central Texas with her husband and young children.

THE NATIONAL POETRY SERIES

The National Poetry Series was established in 1978 to ensure the publication of five poetry books annually through participating publishers. Publication is funded by the Lannan Foundation; the late James A. Michener and Edward J. Piszek through the Copernicus Society of America; Stephen Graham; International Institute of Modern Letters; Joyce & Seward Johnson Foundation; Juliet Lea Hillman Simonds Foundation; and the Tiny Tiger Foundation. This project also is supported in part by an award from the National Endowment for the Arts, which believes that a great nation deserves great art.

2004 Competition Winners

DAVID FRIEDMAN of New York, New York, *The Welcome*
Chosen by Stephen Dunn, to be published by University of Illinois Press

TYEHIMBA JESS of Brooklyn, New York, *Leadbelly*
Chosen by Brigit Pegeen Kelly, to be published by Verse Press

CORINNE LEE of Austin, Texas, *PYX*
Chosen by Pattiann Rogers, to be published by Penguin Books

ANGE MLINKO of Brooklyn, New York, *Starred Wire*
Chosen by Bob Holman, to be published by Coffee House Press

CAMILLE NORTON of Stockton, California, *Corruption*
Chosen by Campbell McGrath, to be published by HarperCollins

PYX

Corinne Lee

PENGUIN BOOKS

PENGUIN BOOKS
Published by the Penguin Group
Penguin Group (USA) Inc., 375 Hudson Street, New York, New York 10014, U.S.A.
Penguin Group (Canada), 10 Alcorn Avenue, Toronto, Ontario, Canada M4V 3B2 (a division
of Pearson Penguin Canada Inc.)
Penguin Books Ltd, 80 Strand, London WC2R 0RL, England
Penguin Ireland, 25 St Stephen's Green, Dublin 2, Ireland (a division of Penguin Books Ltd)
Penguin Group (Australia), 250 Camberwell Road, Camberwell, Victoria 3124, Australia
(a division of Pearson Australia Group Pty Ltd)
Penguin Books India Pvt Ltd, 11 Community Centre, Panchsheel Park, New Delhi–110 017, India
Penguin Group (NZ), cnr Airborne and Rosedale Roads, Albany, Auckland 1310, New Zealand
(a division of Pearson New Zealand Ltd)
Penguin Books (South Africa) (Pty) Ltd, 24 Sturdee Avenue, Rosebank, Johannesburg 2196,
South Africa

Penguin Books Ltd, Registered Offices:
80 Strand, London WC2R 0RL, England

First published by Penguin Books 2005

1 3 5 7 9 10 8 6 4 2

LIBRARY OF CONGRESS CATALOGING-IN-PUBLICATION DATA
CIP data available

Printed in the United States of America

pyx\'piks\ n. [ME, fr. ML *pyxis,* fr. L, box, fr. Gk, fr. *pyxos* box (shrub)] (15c) *1*: a container for the reserved host; *esp*: a small round metal receptacle used to carry the Eucharist to the sick *2*: a box used in a mint for deposit of sample coins reserved for testing weight and fineness

—*Webster's Dictionary*

PYX IS FOR THOMAS: *mirabile visu.*

CONTENTS

III. ASCENSION

IV. EMPYREAN

COMMENTS ON *PYX* BY CORINNE LEE

One of the major strengths of the poetry in *PYX* by Corinne Lee is its original and engaging music. This music is consistent, finely crafted with intention and with perfect melding of subject and theme. Lee's use of line breaks and sentence fragments to establish cadence is purposeful, functional, and controlled. As with any strong, self-confident music, the music ringing throughout *PYX* has the ability to entice its audience, to draw its audience into itself, and by so doing, offer new experiences of the subjects her poems address.

Lee's vocabulary, also inherent to the music, is rich and surprising. A quick scan of her superb titles will attest to this. It's a pleasure to encounter a word not immediately recognized, as may happen occasionally in this book, and to discover it is the right word in sound and meaning, an energetic word, a stunning word used in the right way in the right place.

Lee skillfully interweaves wit, playfulness, and a *joie de vivre* with serious study and meditations. She has taken some common topics—a rocky marriage, love, passion, infidelity, a death, family, and domestic scenes—and rearranged their parts and juxtaposed them in unusual ways with references to art, philosophy, and literature. She has rescued them from cliché and presented them with honesty, depth, and humor through her own created prisms. The poems focusing on infants and children are especially effective and fine in this regard.

In *PYX* the reader will encounter elements of our culture both crass and profound, the crucial and the trivial revealed and experienced anew through the unique music of Corinne Lee's robust language.

—Pattiann Rogers
September 24, 2004

The active forces, within and outside the body, are noble, aristocratic, for they govern, they expand.

—Elizabeth Grosz, *Volatile Bodies*

O Altitudo in the bloodstream swims.

—Conrad Aiken, *And in the Human Heart*

PYX

1 · TERRANEAN

Radical disorder is the key to the functions of humus.

—William Bryant Logan, *Dirt*

[T]he raw materials of a planet dropped
from an unseen quarry. . . .

—Henry David Thoreau, *The Maine Woods*

LYSISTRATA MOTLEY

Even the quitch loves, sashaying
belly-blade to blade-belly

when wind is low. Most days,
we fail to notice
that elusive, Rastafarian

canoodle. The poems
therefore darting away, sunken,
through the halls.

Our words becoming escapes,
not spoor. Why can't
our selves intersect
with the exterior?

Because something is sclerotic,
strung high
in the Burundi
Salvador trees. Where dewdrops

are slaver. Listen up:
The Egyptians jettisoned

a mummy's cerebrum, knowing
the heart should do
all thinking.

MANGANESE VARIATION NO. 2

If the kestrel's nautilus ministrations,
so above,
fail to unclose.

If the landscape
is tattered. Omnipresent, the whiff

of creosote.
My having been flayed
into an angular structure. Keeping it

to the ledges. Conveniently, the fabulous hat
appears

on the bed. Thereafter:
the conjugal lullaby, my hair
reinvented

as your divan. In the barn,
the rusted tractors begin sizzling

into laughter. Is it felicity
that any fantasy
can be made?

ALLEGORY OF VENUS AND THE OLIGARCH

An opening in merlot over coal:
this birthday supper

failsafely mine. Our former nudes observe
from an olive grove. We dip

into lemongrass, coconut lather—mutely
envying the intimate

steam fandango. There is no real conversing
with your fact fiefdom. (Is not distance

the final meal,
because the bullet eliminates the word?)

My navel, nipples, and their ilk
become triangular, stab earthward

like diviners. Our jetty spiraling.
Hello to my new self, bride of hardpan, of dead

watches. Yet offstage, there is a faint, heartening
strain of boogie-woogie. Eureka:

The tin ceiling of you doubles
as a boardwalk? I step.

THE PASSING BY OF ROMEO ANALECT

Love for these children is a bathysphere, my nipples
never recognized
as also being mouths. Concentrate on the static
behind them. Which arena

is currently under rubble? Raggedness? Terror?
Desire? Mature love
strides purposefully by,
decked out like a parade float in zoot suit,

fedora, and wingtips. Sir, do not waste
your ultimata
on secondhand me. My ambition has been combed out,
and Sun

is doing all milking.
My only credo? Never admit
this occasional revelation: *Help me, children,*
for I cannot help myself.

THE EPONYMOUS HEROINE

Her again? Mercy.
She and her silver people

are evermore waiting, lipless,
high above. I'm an umber study,

in contrast—always down
for redesign, a counterfeit solaris.

But take note of what I desire: *Tell me
I'm the one you want.*

The penultimate one you need.
Then do as you please.

Rapidement. Speed
is the next best thing to love,

as water beads, perfecting
while it runs. Let's deny

the omnipresent Apocalypsalooza,
every war's echo of innocents

born limbless. I'll be lust-luscious
and oviparous. Shamed free! Because

there's nowhere we can race to
that's painless.

WHITE FLAG

Yeah, I hang from your nod, but these breeches
are just as fine
as yours. Said Erasmus, my book is *kind of a hand dagger,*
a *little blade*

to help you see that *mortal life*
is nothing but . . . perpetual war. Woe to our
breast-to-breast
lovers' combat—winner hoarding
the spoils. Aw, let's take our tincture

of lavender. Police might suspend, bishops resign!
Then, our Birnam wood—
felled, abandoned to breeze licks—

may be shaved into epicure sheets
of the voluptuous. I concede
that you can tear
at my waist, assemble me
on the ecstatic's shiny platter. But then, you must return
my entirety,

in all its daunting
über-smug (property dreads the thievish
because it was thieved). The lion roars,

upon spying a woman's flesh
between the legs, O *poor lady,*
who hath wounded thee
so deeply?

SLURRY

I'll not be covert
and, thus, your capital. Take your pill: Today
is my cedar
disposition. Only halfway there, neither up

nor down. In our neighbors' fields, snap
peas sweat and slumber, fattening
on gingered sky. Yet I stride sardonic
as acetate, badgers heating
each shoulder. Is this how Nature reveals

herself to Science—
by clawing apart her puffy Oxford,
disclosing breasts that seem,
to him, like grenades? You tell me
there are pipelines

which transport the insoluble
by submerging it
in water. Please, to please, turn on
the tap.

TEN CENTS A DANCE

Send out 100,000,000 electrons,
one by one, and trace
with paint
the pathway
of each journey. When merged,
their terminus art
is a seaweed tangle,
but vaulting.
Cathedral of netting. Unlike
this chapel crate
at the children's hospital. Huzzah,
a priest, milky way
of pretentious statements
against a jazzy background.
Jesters careening
from room to room,
on bicycles made
of hay, while my daughter
wails. Wasn't it the goal
of Venus
to seduce, to gavotte
with Death? Can't begin
the dance. Digitata, nori, alaria,
dulse. Come wrap
this mother and her glue seep, nail
pocks. Wearing her faulty construction
under klieg lights,
for everyone
to see.

LIEDER MÂCHÉ

Everything strafed together. Going over the falls
in a barrel
with the dreamed of, but born awry. Rock oak slats, metal straps.
And liquid thunder,
this bellow which commenced

in night. Outside, scrub pines
are knee deep
in wet. Nutmeg cattails witness
a monarch descend and sup, proboscis
lapping. No map to direct from my bound freefall

to that unhasped exterior—because void
is always interrogating the poem,
because there must be a plummet
before an understand. You see, she was a backyard baby,
unassembled. But nodding lips like coral.
Minute, shell fists,

eyes of seal. After her demise, there was my new imperative:
Next to candids preserving the lost, place
objects she owned and might have loved—
stained bear bib, gummed blanket. For incessant
regard. Yet suddenly
there is a bobbing up

(not anywhere near my doing). Thank you, Bottom.
Thank you, Mud. A wake-walking into a newer world, aflame
like matins. Electric cumulus, schools
of gemmy fish. And look: Here are those jonquils
that sometimes follow a reopening
of hope.

AFTER THE CAVES

The hummingbird is dead, lashed
to this neck. Wings

labial. Framing the scene:
dozens of daisy-

chained, margarine/
gray moths. If born with plenary,

the infant
daughter might have had

a rib like mine.
Instead, this portrait

of woman as table.
Carved by opener

of the body. Surely the nipple,
once pierced,

is stigmata, a brand
of self-made exile?

Clasp me this way, Father.
No, that way.

Let's, uh,
readjust.

OUR LADY OF THE DIVINE SACRUM

Even the picador, gold-threaded chest taut,
trembles
after a time. So I wonder,
Is the architecture
of our affaire de coeur
only presumption, machination? We're atop

the hightowers
of our ardor. The wind, frustrated,
plunges like cormorants
into the hemispheric panes,
our vertebrae gypsum. And the wind

shall win. And we
shall leave each other
to fall. Nothing below us but porpoises, bucking
at the omega

of their unyielding, golden chains. Astride their backs,
we will again ride.
Separately ashore. While thinking the bone
of salvation: *Others*
are lone-dying, and we need
to help them live.

SWIMMER LOST IN LAKE (MIDNIGHT)

Bordering
the ochre bombsite were boutiques—and condominiums,
fin de siècle dandies residing

in each.
For shame, my love, the view we had
from those mullioned windows

at dawn.
Why is it that the best revelations
wake too late (e.g., to achieve a pristine soul, aliases

must be
adopted). We pandered to moral panic. Yet where
can love be made but in a penthouse,

wrapped
in the decisive face paint, multicolored garb
favored by warriors of our tribe? Our not

peering
downward. From life as A Letting Room.
Now a slower and stickier

stroke
begins. Visions of the furred cup. Then an eye
in the plate's center, observing—

11 · MEDIAN

The abyssmal is full in the middle.

—*I CHING*

What should such fellows as I do
crawling between heaven and earth?

—William Shakespeare, *Hamlet*

PETROUSHKAS ON THE BROOK BANK

It was summer, and all the bones were clicking.
Flowers had been scattered
upon your husband waters. Columbine.
Rue. Just after
your slipping in. Beneath proximate cypresses, a tangerine
umbrella (design
circus-ian). Sheltered thereunder, the *vox populi* queried.
Q: *When will the Beyond*
swell
into the accessible?
A: *When there is no more matter*
for us to purchase
or peddle. The dirge-drawn I
began its escape, sidestepping pepperwort
too easily flattened
by leather. Tiptoeing borders
around the faltering
amphibians. Recently overheard: cluster bomb-lettes
are designed
to resemble toys
and candies. But I can no longer ask you (mired in departure),
How to nevermind the generals?

Perchance love
could be lavished, allotted
the same time
as labor. Better not. Bulletin to Lost Ones: The trouble
with thinking
is that it instantly is effluvia, is the past. Yet a relief.
Like water, never failing
to close over.

COCKATRICE AT THE WASHING MACHINE

Forced into peerless distance, briars—
your dismissal

of me has stricken
feral. The scrub countries behind

your fracas eyes
(wishing off with this head?).

My apologies, but no suttee,
no thinking

inside the box. The mechanical swishing
of your garb.

Mine. Navy seeping
into ivory, my vanilla

Madonna tainted. Be warned:
when attempting to clear

your range
of this wolf, you failed

to realize her task
of shrinking

the irksome
herd.

AS BIGFOOT, I INTERPRET
OUR HEYDAY

Our marriage—the arrested
gesture. So this needle
does no stitching. Newborn but lengthy and elastic

is my dope-
stippled horizon. You're entitled to ask, *Will the future*
of our union

be smooth
or shaggy? I can only answer
that we should never
have wed. Yet you require me—always exterior,
always a locus

for wildness. Flattered, I smile.
At you. But then you sniffle
and slump, retreating
the way you do. My palms become paws, holding still,

deep in our crawdad hole. You: an unwitting catfish,
rising from mire like a lily
to my lethal sun. I remain steadfast. Injurious! One foot on earth,

the other at the pharmacist's. Am I Genesis?
Nay, I am the echo of our love.
Lost.

PAST + PAUCITY + H$_2$O

Numbering the willow's leaves,
not these pages. As solace.
Because anyone can read
the entire history
of collision
in our picture. Our last
sea-sand-mud bath, a digging morning,
plump pails, hopscotching
home on stones
that could be true.
At dusk, mussels exploding
from the pot.
Behind every real object,
there is an object
dreamed.
An ambiguous bile color
can pull me back
to that time.
The children bedwetting,
your phobia re stray
parings. Skinflint
embraces. One rule
of the waters:
When a crest
and trough converge,
they cancel each other
into a plane.
Which were you? And I was—?

QUAIL

before my gaze—that of a panopticon, film producer's couch.
So vigilant in its slap-happy
adoration

of you. Our post-prandial, post-love flamingo flush.
Quilt-coddled, we feel
a male wood thrush wheeling, not only outside
the window,
but also within our veins,

woo-warbling chants
like wicks. Beneath his lyrics, your wife's station wagon
bends back, seeking. Returning.
That fine gravel pings
off the road. Fall's leaf smoke slips in,

a vellum gravy
on our tongues. Conceded: The world,
once returned to, will be spiny, a stockade. Why not, instead,
wear paint for attire? We could love each other

in huts of dried mud,
palm thatch. Yet while we fly there, over the boscage,
we look down. One speckled, malt bird
who calls *tut-tut-ee-ay-ee*. And nothing

but pyres.

IN THE LEPROSARIUM

Refusing to concede, the morays
are arcing in, through the window,
snap snap snap snap,
unhinging

the domestic
union. Re libations accelerating
to drunkenness, my grandmother advised,
Drink your liquor wet,
but hide it dry. Done. I'd belong

to Don Juan again, the lost husband,
if only He'd call. He once proclaimed:
The crux
of lovers' conflict, both minor and major,
is that the epic

becomes commonplace. The tragic
becomes cliché. So this sea turtle
weeps to maintain balance,
extruding

salt in balled tears. While watching the ones
like Him—the purely fusiform,
the great whites—

move straightest and fastest
away.

GRISELDA

I. School
II. Manner
III. Mannerism
That has been the footpath
of our love. I've always specialized
in skimming kisses
across the least suitable,

of which you are a prime member—
all for my thrill
of Piccadilly flirt-us. Yet now there is a fontanel,
cooing and crested

with auburn down, filling
my breasts' cleft. Day-old colostrum
like nougat
on her slightly older chin. Both pinnacle and vortex,

she *is*. Will always be. Acknowledged, I can't take a mirage
family's balm-driven weather
with me. So I won't breathe
this stale air,

will deny vipers seethe
around our frame. Sometimes we must playact
beneath mask grins, hide
behind rain.

THE NARROWS

If you're planning on vanishing, you telegraph,
holding my fist, *leave hard.*
Leave hypersonic.
I'm brim weary of your spooked
prance. But I'm too fat and fraudulent
for that. For last night
and my plea,
once again unmet,
for you husbandly thighs, their sandstone
and codex. And for this too pearl morning,
our daughter
with a swallowtail's antenna that shudders, bend-breaks
as she slides
her matchbox closed. Silent witchery. Such casual
harm. I want to be fished
from this airstream
by a picturesque giant, his slingshot aquiver,
and then buttered
with petals. A close second: I snuff crumpled butterfly
with ether, a merciful slaughter.
To ensure observation's
remote kiss. Our child
strokes wings' lemon powder, rubs
dull iridescence on my cheeks,
lips. The nourishment of decadence,
its comfort just before
an end.

A LEPRECHAUN'S LEXICON

is not different from ours, but his worldview
is pregnant, steeped

in large. We want the wee
rattling in ownership's silk purse. But I'm not your fleece,

husband. Nor
am I your flame. If there is no real Possession

or Other, then is everything Merge?
Might as well ask, *What is the shape*

of space? The reply comes off
in our hands. The troubles are these:
    All meaningful fuels are flammable.
    Milked veins are scar rust.
    Love-lost deities are phosphorus, just like us.

And by now, our romance has made the full arc: Soil as factory.
Electronics. Divestiture

of the spirit. Yet the history
of atoms is romantic, so love

can be made on the phone. Why can't you talk quickly?
Disconnect, wait eons,

then hold me like a soul? Ah, your velocity
of unknowing is too slow.

KRAKATOAN

You're a little blue heron, waiting determinedly
for hours
before spearing.
Not possible to flash and thrash

while I'm escaping. My sneaking away
at night,
like fractured royalty. The newfangled solace
of lavascape.

Yet a suspicion that wild dogs
might roam these darkened
and cooling plains,
searching for something fleshy

to tackle. Blessedly, our old cone
at last collapses, causing
most of the island
to fall beneath water.

Nine months later,
only one dun spider, pistachio-eyed,
minute and fragile,
is found.

FAREWELL, OUR VELOCIRAPTOR

I.
Before the Doubter was made known,
we roamed this city's asphalt pastures, basted

in sunlight. Then, our fruit escaped from its sacks
and rollicked in the auto's back expanse. Some bruised.

Some split, seeds gauche and traveling.

II.
Not long after:
a sprouting. Toppling already, a sippy cup was born to seep
on our imperial kelim. Few warned us

about the laundry's half life, hands always descending
into marsh. Fewer still revealed our artistry would sag

like time-heated glass.

III.
Hear ye, hear ye, the sinewy Doubter has arrived, windblown
but raucous. Saber-clawed. It knows that love

is both winnow and burgeon.
Surely, we begin to think,

all revelations have already been spoken. We cannot stop

slumbering on one leg, tipping among daylight.
Thwack. (The infant has learned
that as objects increase

velocity, their mass also increases.)

IV.
We wake, knowing
the only gems now dangle from gray, frayed rattle strings.

Survival demands we convince ourselves that the Doubter,
when met on the other side, is not a beast,
but a blossom. My loves,

we must purchase—quickly—our tickets.

III · ASCENSION

———◆———

The decentered or vanquished subject initiates the possibility of a heightened eroticism and an affirmation of life beyond the hermetic and closed circuit of the subject.

—Judith Butler, *Bodies That Matter*

And rooks in families homeward go,
And so do I.

—Thomas Hardy, *Weathers*

FAILED AMBUSH AGAINST
FLAMINGOES

Stabat Mater: the mother
remained standing. Yet—a lymphatic horizon,
your lips shivering

as if in gelatin. Paper grass-
coconut eggs-a bleating
from others' beaky mouths. And the news

that your too grown daughter has wandered. *Strayed*,
I reassure. *Not forfeited*. Just briefly subsumed
into her self-

mezzotint. While back here
at the corral, only maraschinos
are frolicsome. To cheer we maternal fire-

eaters (pillarbound). Hocus pocus/
crocus, dear friend. So shall we
effervesce? Remember, there was no retreating,

only celebrating, on the long ago days
our wombs, like hyacinths,
became starred.

ALWAYS A STRAPPING APRICOT
CAN BE FOUND

Clamped into ground
like a windswept toad. Through weep-fury, striving
to train an eye

on marriage's waxen promise:
The lovelies are coming,
the lovelies are coming!

Locating comfort: In the Boolean requirement
that I rise, collect, and mix
for baking. And in reasoning that it's impossible
to savor rumcake

while mourning. After all, the past tells
that at any moment, the marital body
can be scratched. Deeply, of course.

To drag forth a sugared bone
of abalone.

EGGBEATER HYMN
(FIFTH IN A SERIES)

Bacon
on Saran. Phantasmagoric,
the muslin rippling
over French doors. (Coarseness
of substances needed,
the violence with which
they once were torn.) Healing all,
the rhythmic striations
of cream
and yolk. Powder
from Zanzibar, consanguinity
of cheddar. And a child
passing the pectin
and elderberries, glistening
on the violet dish.
So what of
the centaur eyes?
Confined
to salt-baked crocks
(at last loving
because they first
were loved). Yes, that fat mug's seam—
crepey, tucked—
is scrotal. Give me
attachment
or give me death.

EXCAVATION

This is an apostasy of the visual. Some paleontological jive.
My children crouched among mobs at a mock dinosaur dig,
exhuming plastic bone Chiclets

of the Cretaceous. Round and about, the parents
applaud. Are the bones of belonging
made from polyurethane? Are blushes still possible?
Mandatory, our denial that any stout, falling rock

can stop our being, breed
a skeletal nation. Hide here. No, here! Nonsense to weep
too soon, too much, but at least

every tear is a lens. Like my shoveling toddlers, I want
the world to be pristine,
of my design—playground wounds like zippers, raptors
that only kiss dumpling hands.
No bogeyman, no cry. Yet every fossil—

our future—is imperfect and as lonesome
as dust. Now my son and daughter run up,
shellacked with muck. Our flesh chooses to embrace and tickle,
its tenderness a mere hint

of Paradise. Longing from below, buried—
our insatiable bones.

CHILDREN'S LITERATURE

The lizard is walking its dog.

Near the bay, where watermelons grow, we snore beneath glass.
Horses knock their wiry muzzles
against the panes. Beetles drop on our flattened cheeks, skid and flip,
flay at the moon.

The bear is talking and slipping
on fishnet hose.

OK, so the purple apples
are firm and highly polished. We see, on their surface,
our reflected lash-less lids, wart-daubed nose—then ponder
eyeliner and surgery.

Almost anything can grow legs and arms,
speak adorably, sing,
and dance. Keep an eye on that ancient loaf
of pumpernickel.

My grandfather placed a dead serpent in formaldehyde soup
in a bottle. It wore a terrycloth tennis wristband—
like a sweater. Its tail
was crammed inside a baby's shoe.

No one ever wrote a book about it.

A CAUTERANT

There vault our naysayers again,
leaping forth

from the universal conundrum.
We need our buoys back.

Let's just choose: No more wasp and whelp.
Only pear. Note
how the black hole

clasps light. And how everything
has its socket

(our little son's head on your clavicle).
Please lift him

and walk. While you're both
still a-slumber. I'll join,
loping alongside. We'll journey together—

to dip our feet
in the holy current, not pull back

when each sole becomes
a fin.

CONQUEST OF BULWARK

Logos
releases her grip. Carts
of executioners
smoking
on the boulevards.
The lover a bygone trickster
with a floured,
livid face. So I'm opening
to effect
a change. To exist
as hollow reed, Pan piped,
or as grass blade
windblown
to whistling.
Not easily, though, does the lumpen
fade, charged through as it is
with nemesis
and lime. And Babylon
refuses
to be stared
down. But then
in comes my child.
Door to abundance.
Thus all things demand,
unprompted,
Seek only
the infant gods.

WHAT OF THE ALLUVIAL PRIESTS

and priestesses, humming
hosannas as my thoughts jigsaw
into jetsam? (Meanwhile, the babies: Whole-
intact. Perfect
as berries, their pulses slipping

into mine.) These days nights of small hands,
glee. Yes, this is best, to be bled
by love. Yet there is no escape
from the dominion of little, its pecuniary parliament
and constant, ocular kisses. The sunset—now, always a teabag,
used, and beneath this deck,
the push-me-pull-you's constant tussle. No longer

the past, a highway once sauntered.
Alone. Nothing now
but surrounding swamp of orchids
and vagueness. I lift
my glass today, nonetheless. Admitted: Both solids
and spaces are being sifted

into sand. But here are these children,
this family, this kingdom. Of rivers
that do not cease, and bend
back into themselves, like fish inserting
into other fish. Hungry—but aqueous,
incarnate. The world
made Jonah.

ABDUCTION CERTITUDES

ABDUCTION OF AMBITION
Why is the other half
of life's algebraic
always bovine, internetted?
Since we reside in a garden,
there is no purpose
but pollen. Admitted: the mosses
have philosophized
for millennia, but they remain
stump-stunted. Hallelujah
for our ragged vegetable plot
and your sacred labor of treehouse
beneath redbud languor,
feathering mesquite. Why strive
for more than this, my love?
Let us be lengthy,
orange when ripe.

ABDUCTION OF UNBRIDLED PASSION
On rose days, our kin
are sugarcane. Honeyed supper rites.
How deftly the familiar
can kindle, but worry me this:
Have our bricklayers completed
all calculations?
Once a hearth is built,
it is never distant. Surely, elsewhere,
all is honeycombed
with entrances
to rapture. And, if able
to touch you, uncensored
by children's yelps,

my fingertips would
be rising lakes. Spilling. Slaking.

ABDUCTION OF YOUTH
Shush, accept my tongue. An apéritif.
An aspirin. Our robes
part to admit the dimming moon.
Late fall. The silver,
fathomless beneath, surfaces
more easily now,
but generally hides—
just as next week's thoughts
lurk within today's, and the antique way
we will someday love
skulks among us now.

ABDUCTION OF DRY TOAST
Cool cereal of domestic dawns,
tepid porridge of dusk. Eyeless
and floating, the grains butting up
against bowls, sinking
from too candied
saturation. Living in soup
and consuming it, like fish.
Do the dimensions
of her world
amaze the sea cow, or
is every estuary
just another larder? Yet offshore
from the familial,
we would be mere driftwood
atop sea skin. Bumping
each other raw, pain-noisemaking
a cappella.

ARCANUM

Even if our arbors have been inverted. Their roots splaying
into solar extremes. Even if they are swaying neatly
from hooks of the stainless. Even if their nests
have fallen and are as empty as unbought cups.

Even if leaves and bark have been scoured.
Somehow, husband, our love always resurrects
after each of our furious defoliations. Watch us on Day Two,
becoming one with the echinoderms. Those round animals

that never convene because they are already, always
speaking in rings with themselves. Day Three:
having no brain but shell petals,
like the sand dollar, we burrow in spaces
between our spiraled bones, each hollow

a spiritualization. We are treading, on Day Four,
sea deep as a story. Day Five, our flesh,

starfish knobby, loses preciousness and regenerates
to repair egressions, to birth our children. Day Six—We vie,
storm tossed, to be carried far, wash-caressed. Crushed

into companionable aggregate of sand. At last we agree,
on Day Seven, to lift. And to rush like beaches in wind—
charging, not walking, off our besotted
and familiar plank.

THE MILKSTONE

In the garden's night country, gin-steeped she
shivers aside
curdled satin, vinyl. But not altering

the body. Among gladioli,
scratching away a grave.
For past garments. Noticing that soil's upper limit

is the boundary between Earth
and sky. While the husband's gummed-up snores,
although within, echo. Buckshot

through the peonies. Below slumbermutters
of the children, she rises, thinking,
People should be viewed

only while they are sleeping.
Or swimming. Like the dugong, treading
sea upright. And pressing in,

with flippers, her nursing
calf. Until home beckons, hailing her
and all mothers

(stripped but stem-vertical).
So they return, elevated but weighty,
resolute as air.

THE TRILOBITE MANIFESTO

Sufi, sushi, you muse. Hush, husband: Those harmonics
and others beg
to conquer. Let's unearth their fusion. Multiple, parabolic,
clustered against
and into each other—a Mongolian bowl dance
of love. My too thin shoulders,
their freight thick
from piecemeal nights, nestle into yours. Every hour,
our newborn has reigned
her spit pulpit. Yet now her jade-ish eyes
are dream-stitched. A nor'easter pours
beyond shade gapes. Shut off
the static, the televised pander. Shut off the super tankersheroesfries.
Shut off the ulterior logicians.
Then love me down, husband, electric sluice. Our breath
like the wind-whipped elms. Our roots falling
to different waters.
The houseplants jungle up, newspapers propagate
on the porch. And after we're spent, we will sculpt
each other from ash
with our selfsame begotten, begetting hands.

LANDSCAPE WITH BOTCHED
SACRIFICE TO FATA MORGANA

Vikings in the coffee, scimitars
in the tea. Choleric, a sugar bowl totters
on sea legs.

Above this inadequate littlest town
(hayseed familial),
scalloped mansions maunder. Perhaps accept

passing visits. To a lone deity (rhapsodic coinage).
With Her sovereign insistence

that kith and kin be forfeited—
because enlightenment shies
from clans, shuns

this surfeit of flesh and blood
in still life
of underfoot marbles-skipping rope-
jacks. Yet if one
of Her crutches falls,

the dreamer wakes. While stirring
warm oolong, so thickly
cupped. Among sierras of clan, fused
rapt. And sweet trumpery
of toys.

FOLLOWING LABOR: ALCHEMY

CALCINATIO (Burning via Fire)
Sculptural with exhaustion. Watching,
again and again, the infant clamp
on one cracked nipple,
then the next. Sepia bedclothes
cocoon, volcanic. This instant
is paralysis.
Will no one come? Will nothing appear?

SOLUTIO (Diffusing into Water)
Alarm clock whirrs
and slaps. As preface
to the coming storm, streetlight shadows
jitterbug, demonic. The infant squalls
over emotions that burr, rise
to descend. This flesh
is a used lake, and you-he-she-they-we-it-all
are to blame. Not?
Hush of the ancients.
Then, as if on a summer sidewalk,
the windows begin
to melt.

SUBLIMATIO (Ascending in Air)
A hallway
unexpectedly speaks
in variations: spokes of sun-dust, reassuring
as nursery rhymes, velvet edges
like evensongs, snappy stanzas
of light and dark. Geometry dazzles.
From the kitchen of familiar,
leagues below, aroma
of the husband's fried potatoes

ascends. Mockingbird dallies.
As the infant sleeps,
frustrated breastmilk runnels branch, web
into satellite visions
of highways.

COAGULATIO (Descending into Earth)
Finally, *a baby* up-looks—owlish, adoring.
The love fall thus begins,
a spectral trumpet vine
worry-glorying downward, twisting
about my neck, tonguing clavicle,
lace-making on my swollen chest. Its open,
blossoming throats. Widening, pressing
into breasts. A tightening and a tugging forth,
El Dorado at last, this
self so roughly milked
into splendor.

IV · EMPYREAN

[W]hat are [we] . . . all rushing towards? Without a doubt, toward becoming-imperceptible. The imperceptible is the immanent end of becoming, its cosmic formula.

—Gilles Deleuze and Félix Guattari, *A Thousand Plateaus*

Why should our bodies end at the skin, or include at best other beings encapsulated by skin?

—Donna Haraway, *Simians, Cyborgs and Women:*
The Reinvention of Nature

UNIQUE FORMS OF CONTINUITY
WITHIN VOID

A chord cannot be held always
or boxed. And a woman can stream milk

for anyone, mugger or mogul, each drop spooling
like grace, like bisque. There was the night

we wed, you feeding me marzipan papaws
with your teeth. Our love

not yet shrouded
by time's daft—but accurate—disguises. The images

of trees, projected on those bodies, formed
exact maps of avenues

both vascular and skeletal. We then knew
one monkey couldn't stop

the show. We then knew a sea anemone
could inch into the throat, become

the throat. Reproducing by fission.
Our flesh awash

with saline. That easily
anyone can become an ocean,

as fractals are just roadmaps
for twinning, after all.

CONVENTIONS OF PARADISE

It is best to be attached
to a firm object, but occasionally
to shift about very slowly. There is no network
of stoppages. Often, you are visited by a food cart

that advertises, *Carnitas-Hamburgers-Eggrolls-Kebob-
Sushi-Pizza!* When the Chieftains
activate the light fantastic, essences cohere,
e.g., All homeless signs echo,

Hungry. Pumpkins are sometimes carved
with maps of the world. If a magnum and Sterno
once transformed any doorway
into a home for one, now, strangers choose

to embrace you, for they are immune
to stinging tentacles. Accept that forever the flocks
of little birds will coil about, merrily singing, *Thrombosis!*
Hey, you could flee, establish a new colony

in a vacant field mouse nest. Yet this web grows stronger
if the captured struggle. Ooh, release to the breath—
it's a window here, just as snow is bread. And the lion
has become the lamb.

TABULA RASA

Consult
your Rapture Preparedness Kit:
nothing will be skeletonized
tonight. This Aegean is waxing
too vast
for one love sloshing
nearsighted
against one shore. (Scrabbled
by gulls and lost kelp,
sand-coarse.) Succumbing, though,
to your domino gaze. Tracery
of maple shoulder moles.
Yet suddenly grasping
your tendency
to overuse "actually."
Annoyed, lofty-feudal,
I'm pronouncing,
Henceforth, I refuse to speak
or be understood.
Your silent aorta,
vena cava.
Mutely acquiescing, considering:
The sea never intended
to be heard.

WHAT WE FAIL TO READ,
IS READING US

My gone love, there are so many paths. Blank
and mute, blind
like worms nosing loam.
Mesopotamian diviners, bewildered,
hunted wisdom by reading them—

studying entrails of sacrificed creatures,
they saw "Palaces of the Intestines"
in which gods revealed futures (both possible
and real). Pressed coil to coil, those bowels would match

cathedral labyrinth mosaics. Worn
into thin troughs by footsteps
of penitents. Mere skin separates the cool marble floors

from pilgrims' hot inner skeins. Walls
mortal depths away
from exterior wonders. Remove that sheath, and all life
becomes probe, electric:

butterflies can dip wings,
soft shards, between jumping muscles;
lovers' fingertips can trace blue veins
of bare heart. Suddenly superfluous,
the one-note melding of skin-on-skin loving,

if lips can burrow
into pearl larynxes, if two spinal cords
can braid into one rapturous,
sparking plait. That all can be, for pure love discards
the rational. (As its pursuit breeds nothing
but monsters.) So, my phantom love,

you may absorb
this without eyes,
without skin: The body
of the beloved is neither clay,
nor glass, nor granite.
Enter.

THY CRADLE IS GREEN

Benedict, your embraces
once were stays. We loved

the June field then, our planar picnic,
Dexedrine clouds whip-skittering
above. But now, after your leaving,

there are rip cords. Penumbras. And ice
that can only report
it harbors air. Two possibilities remain—

A) Zero is gibbous.

Or

B) From the tipping dinghy,
our skeletons lisp, *It was a nice life.*

The answer: A).
Although true love
took the first bus
out of town, there is still singing

through the waters, chiming
in the sheaves. Those trumpets of Jerusalem.

And I a galleon, untethered, each tide
a mecca that knows
and presses this hull.

FILLIPS OF A FRAGMENTED VALHALLA

1. Unable to bear the stain. Or, at the other end of the spectrum,
   to tolerate
   each cell's pivotal kiss. How to be a hive
   in which all of history has been stored?

   Possible refuges: Foulards. Scarabs. Sweetbriar
   at my breasts.

2. Always a daddylonglegs is striding stickily across, mocking
   our veneer. Our nightstand
   will be shedding alpaca this evening. Darling,
   your wet pulses!

   Surrealism: a lyric battle.
   Against this terrestrial sphere
   of surfaces.

3. Typically, any mixture of broken, discordant elements
   is labeled "monster."

   Yet: Echo dismembered—
   by shepherds. Each crumb at last
   truly singing.

4. The decision was made, without great thought, to place
   just a finger (why not all?) into the side
   of every god.

   Nonresponsive.
   Regrettably, everyone has left, in individual
   packets.
   For the moon.

LACUNA

Believe the wind—its ethos
is the flexing instant. A certain element

of the vague and blank. Like my passion for you,
for anyone, which at root

has a wiped slate face, featureless
but for one

keyhole mouth (black, kiss/limitless). The specific
is a desiccant. So, please concede:

Your sex is not merely you,
but also all violets, and our hands have pasts

as feet. We'll then love with enormity,
joining the deer who,

without precision or diction,
lift their heads

from clover and see
straight through you, me.

STRIDING FORTH, THE NEWLY MINTED

The abyss has reasons, hook-dragging
the gaze
to dark. It's in this prairie-breaking café.

Where only plastic populace grin—
avocado-shaped Claus straddling the register top,
Michelin stomach baker clock

on grimed counter. Everyone's heart holes
as big as Herefords. When will you
interrupt the incessant grinding?

Stall my wondering if television
has supplanted
humanity as the axis of energy

in rooms? The dogstars expand. Finally, you saunter
inward. Belly up to my bar. *De profundis*—
Not. Sorry, big sunny bear,

but your shallows
are clotted with minnows. Opal,
translucent, yet small fry nonetheless. No

matter. Just buss me into blue ether,
my treasure, my pet. We'll pretend to be steep,
above this Formica fray. (While our throttle

lasts.) I'm already unfolding
our paradisiacal anthology, its petals of order
and grace.

SUBSTRATUM

Setting paper cups
of Shiraz

at yarrow's edges
for the elves. The cicadas throbbing.

Of god in the body
and the body in god.

Deck chair imprints
like prison bars,

but a husband's lips cupping
my navel. Stamen

tongue. Oceanic, this excess
of *beaux gestes*. Dropped in,

we must sink,
clenching and loosening,

loosening and clenching, until reaching
prehistory's sand.

THE ECSTASY OF SAINT
MÜNCHHAUSEN (BY PROXY)

Marsh fog,
spaghnum glow
of fires
along the shore. Rowing
with molasses paddles
through the apparitions.
Of those winter evenings
your flesh
was diaphany
of lavender singe,
piñon strata. Inscribing
lip bruises (so medicinal)
on your ankle buttons,
shirred soles.
Ah—you're ailing there.
And there. *Absolve me*
says every tongue.
So we did. Like Juno tossing
the eyes of Argus
on the peacock's tail.
Yet our Eden, like all paradises,
was already shapeshifting.
A baobab
of knobs and twists
we could interpret.
But never master.

RISORGIMENTO

All will resurrect, husband—life's film
running
backward. Dead towers shrugging up,
hay greening,

junkyard jalopies
galloping. The war dogs will again
whimper on furred, corduroy
beds, dreaming

of ovations for ovations. There is no pain
comparable
to being awake. Never enough warmth
or embrace,

as if the mother
never uplifted. Thus, after loss, we'll see
each other, not cloaks. Watch
our children

fizzing in glee
as their lungs expand, crimp
with the universal
accordion. Wheezing

in beats, eternal and utter, music
of the spheres.

SELF-PORTRAIT WITH THORN NECKLET AND CROW

Loneliness
of coral. But beyond yonder window, a spoon bends.
Oil slicks proffer Madonnas. And sacristies hold caches
of crutches flung aside
like chopsticks. (Praises for the cawing miraculous, of comic book
    genus.
Exaggerated. Distant. Ridiculous.) Forgive

this crank. Of late, reality coyotes
have been snuffling through my excesses
of grief. (Just read that shoes, belts, purses

continue to be boiled
for food.) Marching, the line
of medicines on the sill. *I have observed,* said the physician,
that the afterbirth, ordinarily unnoticed,
is painful if the infant
was stillborn. Cannot ignore

your peppermint tulips, their filaments, anthers stuttering
before dropping
from the agate cup. Or the unity promise—
that beneath an electron microscope, the hoops

on a baby's tooth replicate
a conifer's rings. Where are the godly towers? Of Elysium,
from which that tissue
of similars can be logged? Natty, harmonic.
All discrepancies so arrogantly braved.

CONSOLATIONS OF BRICOLAGE

The dead: not only celluloid, but also clouded. Yeasty.
Rising uncertainties.
For you, measureless waves
were galloping—
in random directions. Then married.
Into one
random breaker. Of beauty? *Beautiful like the chance*
meeting
of an umbrella
and a sewing machine
on a dissecting table,
promises Lautréamont. That promise
not fulfilled. Your coffin
of rosewood, stooping
satin.
On a table with lion legs and paws. Those legs carved
so that the table
could not just stand, but walk.
With its furniture
brethren. Now trotting.
From rooms—to throng the streets, parks, and beaches
on which
we loved. Surely the internal, enveloped until breathless,
finds a way out?
The external, adrift in loss, finds
a way in? To Arcadia?
My love?

NOTES

"After the Caves"
Title is derived from Helen Frankenthaler's *Before the Caves*.
Remainder of poem alludes to Frida Kahlo's *Self-Portrait with Thorn Necklace and Hummingbird*.

"Children's Literature"
Second line is derived from the children's song "Down by the Bay" (anonymous).

"Consolations of Bricolage"
Based on Eric Heller's *Random Sphere*, a computer graphic generated by algorithms that present scientific phenomena.
"Beautiful like the chance meeting . . ." is from the Comte de Lautréamont's *Chants de Maldoror*.

"Conventions of Paradise"
"Network of stoppages" is a translation of the title of a Marcel Duchamp painting, *Réseaux des stoppages étalon*.

"Landscape with Botched Sacrifice to Fata Morgana"
First line is an adaptation of "Put cats in the coffee, and mice in the tea" from *Alice in Wonderland*.

"The Milkstone"
Indebted to Yannis Ritsos for *So?*

"Past + Paucity + H₂O"
"Behind every real object, there is an object dreamed" is by Jean Baudrillard, *Le Système des objets*.

"Petroushkas on the Brook Bank"
Refers to a Paraskeva Clark painting called *Petroushka*.

"Self-Portrait with Thorn Necklet and Crow"
See Frida Kahlo's *Self-Portrait with Thorn Necklace and Hummingbird*.

"Swimmer Lost in Lake (Midnight)"
Title was sparked by Jennifer Bartlett's *Swimmer Lost at Night (for Tom Hess)*.
Last two lines refer to Meret Oppenheim's *Object* and René Magritte's

Still Life.

"Ten Cents a Dance"
Thanks to Craig Lambert's article "Quantum Art" in *Harvard Magazine*.

"Unique Forms of Continuity Within Void"
Title is based on Umberto Boccaccio's "Unique Forms of Continuity Within Space."

For Kathleen Peirce, gratitude—of the fathomless variety—for her poems, for her example, and for her unstinting encouragement.

Everlasting thanks to Pattiann Rogers for her lyrics and for choosing *PYX*.

I am beholden to the unfailingly kind and generous Paul Slovak, my editor at Penguin Books.

Most of these poems were inspired, albeit in a highly oblique manner, by *Eklektikos*. Thank you, John.

ACKNOWLEDGMENTS

Grateful acknowledgment is made to the following magazines, in which some of these poems—in slightly different form—appeared.

AUGHT—"Abduction Certitudes," "Conventions of Paradise," "Fillips of a Fragmented Valhalla," "Griselda," "Lacuna," "A Leprechaun's Lexicon," "Quail," "Thy Cradle Is Green," "Unique Forms of Continuity Within Void"

Black Bear Review—"Risorgimento"

DIAGRAM—"Past + Paucity + H_2O"

Foam:e—"Lysistrata Motley," "The Narrows," "Ten Cents a Dance"

GutCult—"The Eponymous Heroine," "Slurry," "White Flag"

How2—"Failed Ambush Against Flamingoes," "Landscape with Botched Sacrifice to Fata Morgana"

Many Mountains Moving—"What We Fail to Read, Is Reading Us"

SHAMPOO—"Swimmer Lost in Lake (Midnight)"

Spinning Jenny—"A Cauterant," "Always a Strapping Apricot Can Be Found"

(ıı) **DATE DUE** ̄J

APR - 2 2006

WITHDRAWN

GAYLORD   PRINTED IN U.S.A.